Guess Who
Swims

Adivina quién
nada

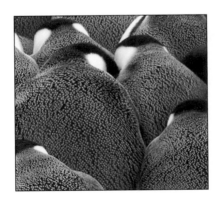

Dana Meachen Rau

 Marshall Cavendish
Benchmark
New York

I swim in the sea.
I can dive very deep.

———◆———

Nado en el mar.
Puedo sumergirme muy profundo.

I eat fish.
I grab them with my *beak*.

———❖———

Como peces.
Los agarro con mi *pico*.

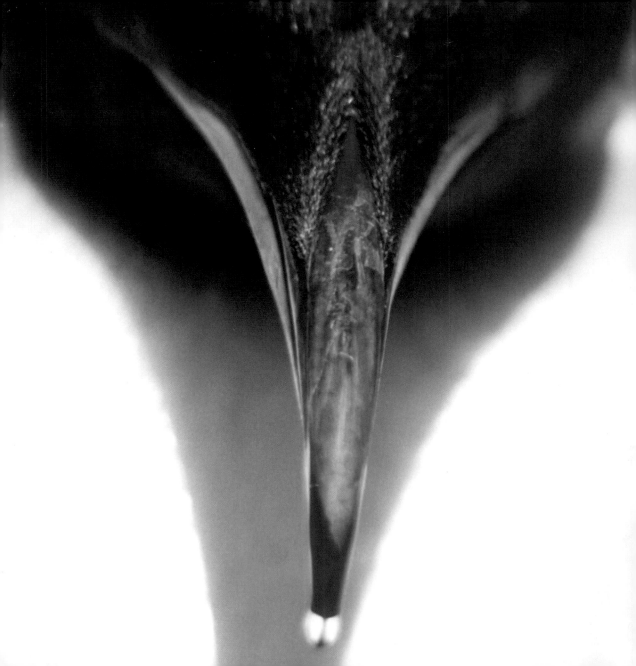

I have black and white feathers.
My feathers keep me dry.

———❖———

Tengo plumas blancas y negras.
Mis plumas me mantienen seco.

I have wings but I do not fly.

❖

Tengo alas pero no vuelo.

My wings help me swim.
I can swim for a long time.

———◆———

Mis alas me ayudan a nadar.
Puedo nadar por largo rato.

My feet help me swim.
My feet help me walk, too.

❖

Mis patas me ayudan a nadar.
También me ayudan a caminar.

I live on the ice.
The ice is cold.

———❖———

Vivo en el hielo.
El hielo es frío.

I live in a group.

My group is called a *colony*.

———❖———

Vivo en un grupo.

Mi grupo se llama *colonia*.

My colony is noisy.
We call to each other.

———◆———

Mi colonia es ruidosa.
Nos llamamos entre nosotros.

I lay one egg.
It has to stay warm.

———❖———

Pongo un huevo.
Debe mantenerse tibio.

My baby is a *chick*.
It has soft gray feathers.

❖

Mi bebé es un *polluelo*.
Tiene plumas grises y suaves.

I slide on my belly.
Who am I?

———————❖———————

Me deslizo sobre mi barriga.
¿Quién soy?

I am a penguin!

———◆———

¡Soy un pingüino!

Who am I?
¿Quién soy?

beak
pico

chick
polluelo

colony
colonia

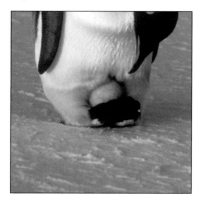

egg
huevo

feathers
plumas

feet
patas

ice
hielo

wings
alas

Challenge Words

beak The sharp, hard, pointy mouth part of a bird.

chick A baby penguin.

colony A group of penguins that live together.

Palabras avanzadas

colonia Un grupo de pingüinos que viven juntos.

pico La boca afilada, dura y en forma de punta de un pájaro.

polluelo Un pingüino bebé.

Index

Índice

About the Author

Dana Meachen Rau is the author of many other titles in the Bookworms series, as well as other nonfiction and early reader books. She lives in Burlington, Connecticut, with her husband and two children.

Datos biográficos de la autora

Dana Meachen Rau es la autora de muchos libros de la serie Bookworms y de otros libros de no ficción y de lectura inicial. Vive en Burlington, Connecticut, con su esposo y dos hijos.

With thanks to the Reading Consultants:

Nanci Vargus, Ed.D., is an Assistant Professor of Elementary Education at the University of Indianapolis.

Beth Walker Gambro is an Adjunct Professor at the University of St. Francis in Joliet, Illinois.

Agradecemos a las asesoras de lectura:

Nanci Vargus, Dra. en Ed. y profesora auxiliar de Educación Primaria en la Universidad de Indianápolis.

Beth Walker Gambro, profesora adjunta en la Universidad de St. Francis en Joliet, Illinois.

Marshall Cavendish Benchmark
99 White Plains Road
Tarrytown, New York 10591
www.marshallcavendish.us

Library of Congress Cataloging-in-Publication Data

Rau, Dana Meachen, 1971–
[Guess who swims. Spanish & English]
Guess who swims = Adivina quién nada / by Dana Meachen Rau.
p. cm. – (Bookworms. Guess who = Adivina quién)
Includes index.
ISBN 978-0-7614-3483-2 (bilingual edition) – ISBN 978-0-7614-2974-6 (English edition)
ISBN 978-0-7614-3458-0 (Spanish edition)
1. Penguins–Juvenile literature. I. Title. II. Title: Nada.
QL696.S473R3818 2009
598.47–dc22
2008015170

Editor: Christina Gardeski
Publisher: Michelle Bisson
Designer: Virginia Pope
Art Director: Anahid Hamparian

Spanish Translation and Text Composition by Victory Productions, Inc.
www.victoryprd.com

Photo Research by Anne Burns Images

Cover Photo by *Animals Animals*/Gerald L. Kooyman

The photographs in this book are used with permission and through the courtesy of:
Peter Arnold: pp. 1, 17, 28TR BIOS Andre Loic; pp. 7, 15, 28BR, 29C Fritz Polking;
pp. 9, 27, 29R S. Muller. *Animals Animals*: pp. 3, 5, 28TL Gerald L. Kooyman;
pp. 11, 21, 28BL Doug Allan/OSF; pp. 13, 29L Johnny Johnson; p. 25 Ben Osborne/OSF.
SuperStock: p. 19 age fotostock. *Corbis*: pp. 23, 28TC Frans Lanting.

Printed in Malaysia
1 3 5 6 4 2